DEVOTIONAL JOURNAL

For Rachel
Christmas 2001
Love from Gwen

A Heart Like His

A DEVOTIONAL JOURNAL BY

BETH MOORE

NASHVILLE, TENNESSEE

Introduction

Of all the characters in Scripture, none appeal to me exactly like David. I guess I identify with him so much because he was such a man of extremes. Nobody loved God with the abandoned passion of David. However, in one of those incredible contradictions, nobody exceeded David for wickedness.

First, David shows me what a vibrant relationship with God can look like—a *Heart Like His*. Then he shows me the evil that dwells in a heart far from God—the evil that dwells in my heart apart from Christ.

In this devotional journal, you will find chronological tidbits from the life of David, following the life of a man with a heart for God. You will find, however, that they are also descriptive of the seasons of our lives. David experienced times of confusion, darkness, loneliness, opposition and fulfillment. Our times include many of the same.

So I encourage you to use this devotion guide as the Spirit leads and your needs dictate. You may want to walk straight through the time line of the shepherd king by following from the first page to the last. We can celebrate his virtues and mourn his failures as we learn from both. On the other hand, you may find yourself drawn to parts of David's life that match your present experience or to give you hope in times of trouble.

In whatever way you choose to interact with one of the greatest lives ever lived, I pray that on these pages you will visit the shepherd-king David, but—even more so—that you will truly encounter the King of Kings. Thank you for your interest in God's precious Word. May the divine Author bless you—as He has blessed me—through my sojourn with the musician king.

I only wish I could be with you to hear the discoveries the Spirit will share with you. I love you.

Beth

CONTENTS

GOD AT WORK

PSALM 78:70-72

He chose David, His servant, and He took him from the sheepfolds of the flock. From behind the nursing ewes He brought him to shepherd Jacob, His people, even Israel His inheritance. So he shepherded them with a blameless heart and guided them with skillful hands.

God chose David. On the surface, the choice made no sense. But God doesn't work on sense; He works on grace.

Do you find God's activity as fascinating as I do? He loves us, calls us, redeems us, and uses us totally because of who He is.

Of David we might think that God called him in spite of the fact that he was a common shepherd. But the facts prove otherwise. God was working in David's life from the beginning…through the invaluable experience of keeping sheep.

EPHESIANS 2:10

We are His making, created in Christ Jesus for good works, which God prepared ahead of time that we should walk in them.

THE DEEPER QUESTION:

Have you discovered the ways God has been working—all of your life—to prepare you for kingdom service? What experiences, lessons, talents, or hurts do you need to present to Him for His use?

_____

_____

_____

_____

_____

_____

_____

_____

_____

_____

_____

_____

_____

_____

_____

_____

_____

_____

_____

Father, thank You for the assurance that You are always at work in my life. Help me see that to follow You never means to throw away who You made me to be.

YOUR POWER SOURCE

1 SAMUEL 16:12-13

He sent and brought him in. He had a bronze complexion, with pleasant eyes and a handsome appearance. The LORD said, "Go ahead and anoint him. He is the one." So Samuel took the horn of oil and anointed him in the presence of his brothers, and the spirit of the LORD rushed upon David and remained from that day on.

The Holy Spirit just can't seem to arrive without power, can He? Even in the life of this little shepherd boy, we see testimony of that power again and again.

David would go on to fell a giant and build a kingdom, but all the good that he accomplished would come from one source—the power of the Holy Spirit.

Samuel's anointing oil may have blurred David's vision when it bathed his eyes that day. But the Spirit's power would help him see things in life that he never dreamed.

ACTS 1:8

You will receive power when the Holy Spirit has come upon you, and you will be My witnesses.

THE DEEPER QUESTION:

You receive the Holy Spirit when you receive Christ (Rom. 8:9), but you do not automatically experience the Spirit's fullness. What specific steps can you take today to live your life controlled by the Spirit?

_____

_____

_____

_____

_____

_____

_____

_____

_____

_____

_____

_____

_____

_____

_____

_____

_____

_____

_____

_____

_____

Lord, I am amazed that You choose to share so personally this life of mine. Today I need Your power. May I surrender to Your leadership.

SMALL FAITHFULNESS

1 SAMUEL 16:19-21

Saul sent messengers to Jesse. "Send me David, your son," he said, "who is with the flock." So Jesse took a donkey, bread, a skin of wine, and one young goat; and he sent them to Saul by David, his son. David came to Saul and presented himself as his servant. Saul liked him very much, and David became his armor-bearer.

What should you do when God has called you but you don't know what to do next? After David was anointed by Samuel, he returned to caring for his father's sheep.

Mark this down, then, as a good principle: Keep studying God's Word and listening to His voice; but while you're listening, take care of the responsibilities He has given you.

Looking back at years of ministry, I have often seen God use that kind of small faithfulness to accomplish more than the great things of which we dream.

MATTHEW 25:23

"Well done, good and faithful slave! You were faithful over a few things; I will put you in charge of many things."

THE DEEPER QUESTION:

In what small things are you being faithful? Can you be fulfilled if God always uses you in ways the world considers small? Why are there no large or small jobs with God?

_____

_____

_____

_____

_____

_____

_____

_____

_____

_____

_____

_____

_____

_____

_____

_____

_____

_____

_____

_____

Father, my ego calls out for recognition, but Your word says that the kingdom belongs to the meek and faithful. Teach me to be faithful in the small things that I may be worthy of whatever You give me to do.

ARTIST AND WARRIOR

1 SAMUEL 16:17-18

Saul said to his servants, "Choose me a man who can play well, and bring him to me." Then one of the servants answered, "There's a son of Jesse, the Bethlehemite, that I've seen. He can play, and he's a mighty warrior, a soldier, skilful in speech, with a pleasing appearance. Also, the LORD is with him."

David had the tenderness and sensitivity of an artist. He was a musician and a songwriter whose comforting melodies truly ministered to King Saul's aching soul.

Yet we are also told he was a warrior, brave and strong. The fingers that gently plucked the strings of a harp could wind fiercely around a sling or a sword.

Tenderness and strength are not exclusive terms. You see them both in David. And in Christ. One without the other leaves an individual lacking wholeness.

2 SAMUEL 23:1

This is David, son of Jesse, speaking ... the anointed of the God of Jacob, the sweet psalmist of Israel.

THE DEEPER QUESTION:

What qualities do you most value—tenderness or strength? In which direction do you lean? What can you do to develop either the sensitive or the risk-taking side of your personality?

Father, I pray that You will teach me to value tenderness and strength in all Your children, male or female, even as You teach me to rely upon Your Son, the essence of all strength.

More of You, Less of Me

1 Samuel 10:9-11

when Saul turned his shoulder to walk away from Samuel, God transformed him, giving him a different heart. . . . when they arrived there at Gibeah, indeed, a band of prophets met him. Then the spirit of God came suddenly upon him, and he prophesied in their midst. . . . Everyone asked each other, "Is Saul also among the prophets?"

A changed heart is the absolute requirement for kingdom service, but a changed heart does not mean a perfect heart. It must be maintained in order to grow in God's direction.

Saul's root problem remained. Just as he had been found hiding among the baggage when the time came for him to be anointed king, he continued to be more concerned about himself and what others would think.

Only God can change a heart, but you must choose whether to give it to Him. Self-consciousness is the opposite of God-consciousness.

Galatians 1:10

Am I now trying to win the favor of people, or God? . . . If I were still trying to please people, I would not be Christ's slave.

THE DEEPER QUESTION:

In what ways can you rejoice because God has changed your heart? In what ways are you still "trying to please people"? What can you do today to be less self-conscious and more God-conscious?

_____

_____

_____

_____

_____

_____

_____

_____

_____

_____

_____

_____

_____

_____

Father, allow me opportunity to humble myself. Teach me one skill that will make me more conscious of You and less conscious of me.

FEARLESS FAITH

1 SAMUEL 14:6,10

Jonathan said to the young man carrying his gear, "Come on! Let's cross over to the garrison of those uncircumcised men. Perhaps the LORD will act through us, for nothing can prevent the LORD from bringing salvation, whether He works through many or a few.... The LORD has given them into our hands."

In one of the great statements of faith backed by action, Jonathan and his armor-bearer challenged the Philistine detachment holding the pass at Micmash. God showed them they should attack, so they climbed up to the soldiers, killed twenty men, and the Israelites won a great victory.

Jonathan knew the Lord could save, no matter who or how many were fighting the battle. His only question was whether God would choose to do it through them that day. His faith in God's strength and determination stood solidly. God could do anything!

LUKE 18:27

"What is impossible with men is possible with God."

THE DEEPER QUESTION:

How would it affect your life today if you thoroughly, completely believed Jonathan's words—that "nothing can prevent the LORD from bringing salvation, whether He works through many or a few."

_____

_____

_____

_____

_____

_____

_____

_____

_____

_____

_____

_____

_____

_____

_____

_____

_____

_____

_____

_____

_____

_____

Lord, like the father of the demon-possessed boy (Mark 9:24), I cry out to You today. I really do believe, but I need You to help my unbelief.

Giant Courage

1 Samuel 17:26,32

David said to the men who were standing by him . . . "who is this uncircumcised Philistine, that he should insult the armies of the living God?" . . . David said to Saul, "No man's courage should fail on account of him! Your servant will go and fight with this Philistine."

As his countrymen cowered in fear, David saw the situation differently. A person who fears God has no reason to fear anything else.

On the other hand, fear becomes a way of life for the person who does not fear God. David feared God, so he did not fear Goliath. Saul did not fear God, so he feared the opinions of others, the enemy, and even a loyal young boy who played the harp.

If only Saul had known this: No giant will ever match a big God with a little rock.

1 Samuel 17:47

"The battle is the LORD'S, and He'll deliver you into our hands."

THE DEEPER QUESTION:

What are your giants? More importantly, what can defeat your giants? I encourage you to follow the example of David. For today, trust your battles to the Lord—these battles . . .

Father, You know how intimidating my giants appear to me. Give me the perspective to measure them, not against my own strength, but against Yours.

WEARING SAUL'S ARMOR

1 SAMUEL 17:38-39

Saul clothed David in his warrior's garments and put a bronze helmet on his head. Then he clothed him with armor. David strapped on his sword over his garment and tried to walk, because he had not tested them. Then David said to Saul, "I can't go in these, since I haven't tested them." And David took them off.

When David volunteered to fight the giant, Saul dressed him in the king's armor. Imagine that picture: a young shepherd boy, dressed in the armor of a middle-aged king twice his size.

Is it any wonder David could hardly walk, let alone fight? David made the wise choice to say, "This just isn't me."

Our attempts to copy somebody else are like wearing Saul's armor. Have you tried to wear Saul's armor? It fits miserably. God has made us to be who we are, not who somebody else is.

1 SAMUEL 17:50

David overpowered the Philistine with a sling and a stone. He struck him down . . . although David had no sword in his hand.

THE DEEPER QUESTION:

You have all sorts of situations that tempt you to try to be someone other than who you are. Recall a time when you tried to wear Saul's armor. What can you learn from that experience?

_____

_____

_____

_____

_____

_____

_____

_____

_____

_____

_____

_____

_____

_____

_____

_____

Father, I know You created me to be myself, not to imitate someone else. Remind me today to be true to You by being myself.

TRUE FRIENDS

1 SAMUEL 18:1,3-4

Jonathan committed himself to David. Jonathan loved David as much as his own life. . . . Jonathan made a covenant with David because Jonathan loved him as much as his own life. Jonathan took off the robe he was wearing and gave it to David, together with his warrior's garment, his sword, his bow, and his belt.

Jonathan's expressions of love and friendship toward David paint one of the most beautiful portraits of covenant in the Word of God. Jonathan gave David his royal regalia—his robe and his warrior's garment—and placed it on David, symbolizing that David would be king over Israel instead of him.

He was so determined that the throne be occupied by God's chosen instrument that he offered everything he had. Jonathan sacrificed himself, acknowledging David as prince of the Hebrew nation—a position he could have jealously and vehemently claimed as his own.

1 SAMUEL 20:17

Again Jonathan swore to David in his love for him, because he loved him as he loved his own life.

THE DEEPER QUESTION:

Paul wrote that God's kind of love is not self-seeking (1 Cor. 13:5). We all long to be loved with a such a selfless love, but what can you do today to become a lover like Jonathan?

_____

_____

_____

_____

_____

_____

_____

_____

_____

_____

_____

_____

_____

_____

_____

_____

_____

_____

Dear Father, develop the spirit of Your Son in me that I may love as Jonathan loved without selfish thoughts or motives.

THE GREEN-EYED MONSTER

1 SAMUEL 18:7-9

As the women danced, they sang: "Saul has struck down his thousands, but David, his tens of thousands!" This song made Saul furious and very upset. He said, "They've credited to David tens of thousands, but to me they've credited only thousands. All he needs now is the kingship!" So Saul began regarding David with suspicion from that day on.

In stark contrast to Jonathan's self-sacrifice and solemn allegiance, Saul regarded David as the ultimate threat.

The praise of the people directed at David planted a seed of jealousy in Saul—so extreme that he sent David to fight in the army, hoping he would come to harm there.

Few experiences are more miserable than being the subject of someone's unleashed jealousy. Perhaps the only thing worse is being the one in whom the jealousy rages. Saul began a descent into jealousy that would finally destroy everything he cared about.

1 SAMUEL 18:29

Saul became even more afraid of David, and he remained David's enemy the rest of his life.

THE DEEPER QUESTION:

Envy can poison the very wellspring of your life. How do you feel when envy strikes? Prayerfully describe all the weapons in your arsenal to fight against envy.

_____

_____

_____

_____

_____

_____

_____

_____

_____

_____

_____

_____

_____

_____

_____

_____

_____

_____

_____

_____

_____

Lord, You show such pure love, but I struggle with wanting the attention others receive. Teach me to daily crucify my envious thoughts.

Ragged-Edge Emotions

1 Samuel 19:4-5

"May the king not sin against his servant David," he said, "since he hasn't sinned against you, and since his actions have been greatly to your benefit. He took his life in his hand when he struck down the Philistine, and the LORD gave a great victory to all Israel. . . . So why should you sin against innocent blood by killing David for nothing?"

Jonathan risked his own life for David. With well-chosen words he calmed Saul's jealous rage, but it returned with a vengeance. Without God's intervention, we can offer only a small bandage to someone hemorrhaging from uncontrolled emotions.

Our emotions, when negatively ignited, can be more powerful than we are. Our best recourse when negative emotions begin controlling us is to fall before the throne of grace and seek God! Take solace in the fact that Christ knows how it feels to be tempted by feelings (Hebrews 2:18; 4:15).

1 John 4:18

There is no fear in love; instead, perfect love drives out fear. . . . The one who fears has not reached perfection in love.

Ho⟨...⟩ otions are raging? What can you do to
reg⟨...⟩ ions—even your most out-of-control
em⟨...⟩

(inset bookmark)

12

**50th
Wedding
Anniversary**

Of all life's
blessing
Very few
Are meant to last
A life time
through,
But love
With all its
joys and tears
Grows only
deeper
Throughout
the years.

**Samuel &
Mary Vazquez**

April 1951– 2001

Lo⟨...⟩ derstand my out-of-control emotions.
Te⟨...⟩ before I dump them on others.

How the Kingdom Crumbles

1 Samuel 19:19-20,23

It was reported to Saul, "Look, David is at Naioth in Ramah." So Saul sent messengers to take David. But when they saw the company of prophets prophesying . . . the Spirit of God came upon Saul's messengers; and they too began to prophesy. . . . So he went there, to Naioth in Ramah; and the Spirit of God came even upon him.

When a group of evil men met a group of godly men, godliness won. How encouraging to remember that the Spirit of God is more powerful than the spirit of wickedness!

Love is more powerful than jealousy, godliness is more powerful than wickedness, and the Spirit of God is more powerful than anything!

As 1 John 4:4 reminds us, "the One who is in you is greater than the one who is in the world." The best laid plans of kings and queens crumble under the mighty Spirit of God.

Luke 11:20

"If I drive out demons by the finger of God, then the kingdom of God has come to you."

THE DEEPER QUESTION:

Do you sometimes feel like nothing can be done for some situation in your life? Remember that God has only to command something and it will come to pass. How can such confidence affect you today?

_____

_____

_____

_____

_____

_____

_____

_____

_____

_____

_____

_____

_____

_____

_____

Father, You are the unparalleled King of the universe, but in everyday matters I so easily forget. Please remind me to trust You today.

Uncommon Friendship

1 Samuel 20:2-4

[Jonathan] answered, "God forbid! You will not die." ... David vowed persistently, "Your father certainly knows of the regard you have for me, so he thinks, 'Jonathan must not know this, or he would be grieved.' But as the LORD lives and as you yourself live, there is only a step between me and death." Jonathan said to David, "Whatever you say, I'll do for you."

True friends can speak their minds without fear. Imagine the tone David used with Jonathan when he demanded to know why Saul was seeking to kill him. David's words suggest nothing less than panic.

Yet Jonathan could easily have received David's words as an insult. You can almost hear them shouting at each other. David came close to holding Jonathan responsible for Saul's actions, and Jonathan came close to getting defensive.

But allowing others to speak their fears even when we can't understand is characteristic of genuine friendship.

1 Samuel 20:13

"May the LORD punish me and do so severely if my father intends to do you harm and I don't inform you."

THE DEEPER QUESTION:

How do you respond when a friend confronts or even accosts you? What growth in your character would enable you to respond without getting defensive? How can you learn to avoid feeling threatened?

_____

_____

_____

_____

_____

_____

_____

_____

_____

_____

_____

_____

_____

_____

_____

_____

_____

Father, help me to be so secure in You and so unselfish toward others that I could follow Jonathan's example. Teach me to be an uncommon friend.

Fast-Acting Pain Relief

1 Samuel 21:10-11,13

David rose and fled that day from Saul, and he went to Achish the king of Gath. The officials of Achish said to him, "Isn't this David, the king of the land?... So he altered his behavior and began acting like a madman while he was with them. He made marks on the doors of the gate and let his spittle run down his beard.

We see a new, creative, and shrewd side of David in this situation. Not only was he a harpist and a warrior, he could have won an Oscar for best actor!

Some people act for pleasure. Others act for money. But David was acting for his life. And he pulled it off, too.

You may be wondering why the men of Gath didn't kill him on the spot. David knew the pagan people of his day. They were terrified of a madman and far too superstitious to harm one. Apparently, David wasn't just sheep-smart, he was street-smart.

Luke 12:11-12

"Don't worry about how you should defend yourselves or what you should say. For the Holy Spirit will teach you at that very hour."

THE DEEPER QUESTION:

Do you worry about the what-if situations? How has God supplied the words you needed in the past? Can any situation you may face in the unknown future be beyond God's ability to meet your need?

_____

_____

_____

_____

_____

_____

_____

_____

_____

_____

_____

_____

_____

_____

_____

_____

_____

Father, make me aware of the constant reminders of Your presence in my life. Help me have Your assurance, no matter my circumstances.

For Crying Out Loud

Psalm 6:2-5

Be gracious to me, LORD, for I am weak; heal me, LORD, for my bones are trembling. My whole being is shaking with terror; as for You, LORD—how long? Return, LORD, and rescue my life; deliver me because of Your faithful love. For there is no mention of You in death. Who will praise You in the grave?

Can you imagine the devastation David must have experienced having all his hopes dashed to pieces, being forced to live on the run from a wildly jealous king? He had not only left his home; now he'd even run from his home away from home.

And although he had found a cave in which to hide, it was no refuge because no one was there who cared personally for him.

Ultimately, David would rise above these circumstances. Yet many times we, like David, must be brought down by God to a lowly position before He can raise us up to stand on solid ground.

Psalm 57:2

I cry to God Most High, to the God who avenges me.

THE DEEPER QUESTION:

Think of a time of devastation in your life, a time when you truly didn't know if you'd be able to make it through. Did you cry out to God? In what ways do you see that He has responded to your cries?

_____

_____

_____

_____

_____

_____

_____

_____

_____

_____

_____

_____

_____

_____

_____

_____

Father, I know that times of distress and devastation come in this life, but keep me ever close in the midst of them, and teach me, Lord, to cry out to You.

WHEN IT RAINS, LET IT POUR

PSALM 62:5-8

Rest only in God, O my soul, for from Him my hope comes. He alone is my rock and my deliverance; He is my refuge; I will not stagger. Upon God rests my salvation and my glory; my refuge is in God, the rock of my strength. Trust in Him at all times, O people; pour out your hearts before Him. We have God as a refuge.

Few of us would argue about prayer being the proper response in our crises, but we often don't perceive prayer as being the most practical response. We think, "God can save me from my sins but not from my situation."

David also poured out his complaint to God. He freely told God his troubles.

I am convinced this is one of the major contributors to David's godlike heart: He viewed his heart as a pitcher, and he poured everything that was in it on his God, whether it was joy or sadness, bitterness or fear.

PSALM 62:1

Only because of God does my soul rest; from Him my deliverance comes.

THE DEEPER QUESTION:

What troubles do you need to pour out to God? Do you fear He may be tired of hearing? Remember—David poured some of the same troubles out to God for years and decades. You can, too.

_____

_____

_____

_____

_____

_____

_____

_____

_____

_____

_____

_____

_____

_____

_____

_____

_____

_____

_____

Father, remind me today that You care about every aspect of my life. Teach me to pour my heart out to You and to trust You more each day.

Helpful Reminders

Psalm 16:7-10

I will bless the LORD who counsels me; my mind admonishes me even at night. I keep the LORD before me always. Because He is at my right hand, I will not be shaken. Therefore my heart is glad and my spirit rejoices. My body also will rest securely, because You will not abandon my soul to the grave; You will not allow Your godly one to see the pit.

David did not just pour out his emotion; he also rehearsed his trust in God. David was so exhausted that he feared he would become negligent in his alertness to the snares his enemies set for him.

So his prayer to God also became a reminder to himself: "Because you are at my right hand, I will not be shaken."

Prayer is for our sake as much as it is for God's pleasure. When I see the words I've written in my journal extolling the mighty virtues of God, I am reminded of His constant activity on my behalf, and my faith is strengthened.

John 14:26

"The Holy Spirit, whom the Father will send in My name, will teach you all things and remind you of everything I have told you."

THE DEEPER QUESTION:

what acts of God can you rehearse to Him today? How has he shown Himself faithful? Remember—when you rehearse His faithfulness, you feed your faith.

_____

_____

_____

_____

_____

_____

_____

_____

_____

_____

_____

_____

_____

_____

_____

_____

Father, when my heart grows faint and I fear that You do not hear me, teach me to rehearse Your faithfulness and to lean on You.

Getting Past Put-Downs

Psalm 52:5-7

God will demolish you forever. He will snatch you up and tear you from your tent; He will uproot you from the land of the living. The righteous will view it in awe. They will laugh at him: "Here's the young man who does not make God his refuge. He has trusted in the abundance of his riches; he takes refuge in his own destruction."

Psalm 52:7 tells us something vile about the ego of King Saul: He took "refuge in his own destruction," growing strong by destroying others.

Have you ever known anyone who made him or herself feel bigger or better by putting others down? Putting others down to build ourselves up is perhaps the ultimate sign of gross insecurity.

Thankfully, most people with such insecurity don't have the kind of power Saul had to physically destroy people. However, if we allow our insecurities to govern our lives, we can become destroyers just as certainly as he did.

John 21:21-22

[Peter] said to Jesus, "Lord—what about him?" . . . Jesus answered, "What is that to you? As for you, follow Me."

THE DEEPER QUESTION:

Do you sometimes seek to build yourself up by tearing others down? How do you feel about yourself or someone else when they do the same to you?

Father, my ego and desire for recognition sometimes blind me to my faults and to the virtues of others. Teach me to honor You by honoring other people.

DOUBLE CHECKING

1 SAMUEL 23:2-4

The LORD answered. "Attack the Philistines and save Keilah." But David's men said to him, "Look, we're afraid here in Judah. How much more will we be if we go to Keilah against the Philistine ranks?" David asked the LORD again, and the LORD answered him, "Rise, go down to Keilah, because I am going to give the Philistines into your hand."

When David was uncertain about his direction, he went back to God for confirmation. If David was misunderstanding God, many lives could be lost. It wasn't that David was doubting God when he asked Him a second time, but because he needed to be certain.

In the same way, you might ask God to reconfirm His direction, not because you doubt God's Word, but because you question your own understanding. To doubt God in the face of clear direction is disobedience, but to double-check your understanding and interpretation of God's will is prudent.

JOHN 7:17

"If anyone wants to do His will, he will understand whether the teaching is from God or if I am speaking on My own."

THE DEEPER QUESTION:

What do you do when you are uncertain? Do you trust God enough to double-check your directions? Are you comfortable enough in His grace to ask Him honest questions without fear of offending Him?

Father, teach me to trust You so totally that I can come before You boldly with my questions and my struggles.

Sweet Revenge?

1 Samuel 24:2-4

Saul took three thousand chosen men out of all Israel, and went in search of David and his men. . . . There was a cave, and Saul went in to relieve himself. . . . David's men said to him, "Here is the day the LORD told you about: 'Look, I am going to deliver your enemy over to you, for you to do to him what seems best to you.'"

Amazing! David resisted revenge after all Saul had done to him! After all the lives Saul had taken! In spite of all that he had done, David continued to have a tenacious belief that he must respect God's anointed king.

After Saul left the cave, David called to him from a safe distance. He offered the fact that he had just spared Saul's life as proof of his loyalty. David's men must have thought he was crazy! But David apparently chose to risk man's disapproval over God's, regardless of the consequences.

Romans 12:19

Leave room for His wrath. For it is written: "Vengeance belongs to Me; I will repay," says the Lord.

THE DEEPER QUESTION:

when have you wanted to feel the satisfaction of avenging yourself? Has God given you reason to think that He can't handle things better Himself?

Lord Jesus, give me the strength today to bring my hurts to You and refrain from seeking any justice on my own. Thank You for being completely trustworthy.

Spoken Very Gently

1 Samuel 25:10-12

Nabal answered David's servants, "Who is David? . . . Should I take my bread and my water and my meat that I've slaughtered for my shearers and give it to men from—I don't know where?" So David's young men went back the way they had come. When they arrived they reported all of these things to him.

Nabal almost brought disaster on himself and his entire household. Fortunately his wife, Abigail, had better sense. She prepared gifts and hurried to intercept David before he and his men brought retribution to her husband and household.

When she reached David, she bowed before him, asking him to forgiver her wicked husband. Abigail continued by praising David and making her case for him to spare her household. She asked him to accept her gift of thanks. Truly she enacted the words of Proverbs 15:1—"A gentle answer turns away rage."

Colossians 4:6

Your speech should always be gracious, seasoned with salt, so that you may know how you should answer each person.

THE DEEPER QUESTION:

Are you more inclined to be gentle like wise Abigail or foolish like Nabal? How do you react when someone insults or offends you? What would you like to change about the way you usually respond?

_____

_____

_____

_____

_____

_____

_____

_____

_____

_____

_____

_____

_____

_____

_____

_____

Father, teach me the art of restraint, allowing You to fight my battles for me. Give me grace to pour oil on troubled waters.

DEADLY DISCOURAGEMENT

1 SAMUEL 27:1,8-9

David said to himself, "I am now sure that I'll be destroyed someday by the hand of Saul. The best thing for me is to escape to the land of the Philistines." ... David and his men went up and raided. ... Whenever David attacked a country, he would not leave a man or woman alive, but he would take flocks and herds, donkeys and camels, and clothing.

What happened to David? Why was he taking up an alliance with the enemy? Why was he on such a rampage with every surrounding village?

Life on the run obviously took its toll. Fear, frustration, and exhaustion apparently caused David to experience hopelessness, perhaps even depression and panic. Possibly he was driven to the point of paranoia.

You can hear the downward spiral in his thinking. David was convinced he would be destroyed. And what do we often do when we feel that way? We unwittingly try to take others with us. Scary, isn't it?

2 CORINTHIANS 4:11

We who live are always given over to death because of Jesus, so that Jesus' life may also be revealed in our mortal flesh.

THE DEEPER QUESTION:

How do negative thoughts prey on your mind during discouraging times? How can such times lead you toward Christ instead of away from Him?

_____

_____

_____

_____

_____

_____

_____

_____

_____

_____

_____

_____

_____

_____

_____

_____

_____

_____

_____

Father, in times of discouragement, dark thoughts close in. Give me grace and wisdom to seek intimacy with You during such times.

GOD, ARE YOU HIDING?

PSALM 10:1-3

Why do you stand at a distance, LORD? Why do you hide in times of distress? In arrogance the wicked hotly pursues the poor; may they be caught in the schemes they have plotted. For the wicked boasts about his soul's craving, and the greedy curses and despises the Lord.

David felt that God was far away and hidden in his time of trouble. And he was wondering why.

At this point David serves as an example of what happens when we focus more on our battles than on God. Our enemy appears bigger, we appear weaker, and God appears smaller. Everybody loses.

So beware! Long term battle can cause impairment to your spiritual vision if your eyes focus anywhere but up! God knows when you're almost ready to give up or give in. Keep telling Him. Stay in His Word. Keep claiming His promises.

LUKE 12:32

"Don't be afraid, little flock, because your Father delights to give you the kingdom."

THE DEEPER QUESTION:

When have you felt that evil was prevailing? How has God shown you that He is still on His throne? How has He demonstrated to you His faithfulness?

Lord, sometimes this world tempts me to believe that evil prevails while the righteous perish. Teach me to keep my eyes focused on You in all circumstances.

UNFORGETTABLE

PSALM 10:11-14

He says in his heart, "God has forgotten; He has hidden His face; He will never see." Arise, LORD; lift up Your hand, O God. Do not forget the poor. Why has the wicked despised God? He says in his heart, "You will not require an account." But You do see trouble and grief! You observe this in order to take the matter in Your hand.

Sometimes circumstances look as if God has forgotten His children. But He has not forgotten.

He has seen your battles. He has gathered your tears and blotted your brow. He knows those who have treated you unfairly.

For a time David let the conflict he experienced cloud his calling. He remembered the day Samuel had anointed him king, but forgot that God always finishes what He begins. In seasons like his, we must remember to always stand in God's Word and ever resist the temptation to panic.

PSALM 11:3

When the foundations are destroyed, what will the righteous do?

The Deeper Question:

What kinds of experiences have caused your foundations to tremble? What have you learned from your times of trembling? How can you better prepare yourself for such times?

_____

_____

_____

_____

_____

_____

_____

_____

_____

_____

_____

_____

_____

_____

_____

_____

_____

_____

Father, sometimes my foundations shake and I fear in my heart that You have forgotten me. Hold me close in those times, Lord, and keep me crying out to You and not in despair.

When God Is Silent

John 4:15-18

"Sir," the woman said to Him, "give me this water so I won't get thirsty and come here to draw water." "Go call your husband," He told her, "and come back here." "I don't have a husband," she answered. "You have correctly said, 'I don't have a husband,'" Jesus said. "For you've had five husbands, and the man you now have is not your husband."

At one point in his life, Saul became desperate for a word from God, but God remained silent.

We know that God never responds haphazardly, nor does He withhold an answer without regard. Then why is God silent at times? One reason can be our sin.

I can vividly remember times in my life when God seemed silent, and I realized He was waiting on me to confront and confess certain sins in my life. His silence suggested, "I will not go on to another matter in your life, my child, until we deal with this one."

1 John 1:9

If we confess our sins, He is faithful and righteous to forgive us our sins and to cleanse us from all unrighteousness.

THE DEEPER QUESTION:

Have you experienced times when God was silent because you refused to take the next step with Him? For what other reasons is God sometimes silent?

_____

_____

_____

_____

_____

_____

_____

_____

_____

_____

_____

_____

_____

_____

_____

_____

_____

_____

_____

_____

_____

_____

Father, I struggle to know Your presence continually in my life. Teach me to listen patiently for Your voice and to Your Word. Make me always willing to follow and to wait upon You.

PREPARE TO DIE

1 SAMUEL 28:17-19

"The LORD has torn the kingdom from your hand and given it to your neighbor—to David. Just as you did not obey the LORD and did not carry out His wrath on Amelek, so the LORD has brought this situation on you today. In addition, the LORD will also deliver Israel along with you over to the Philistines. Tomorrow you and your sons will be with me."

I find myself wishing that even Saul's life had an ultimately happy ending. When Samuel said, "Tomorrow you and your sons will be with me," we do not know what Samuel meant. He may have simply meant, "You are about to die." Or he may have meant that Saul and his sons would join Samuel among the redeemed.

I'd like to think that Saul and his sons took the opportunity to settle business with God, knowing of their imminent demise. Sometimes the most merciful thing God can do in a rebellious person's life is to let him know he is going to die so he can beg for mercy.

LUKE 12:20

"You fool! This very night your life is demanded of you. And the things you have prepared—whose will they be?"

The Deeper Question:

Who do you know who isn't ready to face eternity? Are you praying for them daily? What can you do to share the Gospel with them? Are you unashamed to say it? Do you believe God's Spirit can get through?

Lord, the busyness of life distracts me. Remind me that we must soon stand before You. Give me opportunities and courage to witness for You today.

SOMEONE TO BLAME

1 SAMUEL 30:3-4,6

When David and his men came to the city,
they discovered that it had been burned down
and that their wives, sons, and daughters
had been taken captive. Then David and the
people who were with him wept.... This was a
desperate situation for David since the people
were talking about stoning him.... But David
strengthened himself in the LORD his God.

Hurting people often find someone to blame. When we've suffered a loss, we (like David's men) often look for stones to throw—and someone at whom to throw them.

David also suffered the loss of his family. He did not know if he would ever see them again. He had taken many lives. I'm sure he assumed his enemy would not blink an eye at taking the lives of his wives and children.

David cried the same tears the other men cried, but because they needed someone to blame, they focused their anger on him.

GENESIS 50:20

"You truly meant to cause me misfortune,
but God meant it for good in order to bring
about what has now happened."

THE DEEPER QUESTION:

What kinds of situations bring out the blamer in you? How can you deal with feelings of anger and the desire to blame others? What aspect of your relationship with God can help you overcome blame?

Father, teach me to trust Your wisdom and goodness so that my reflex will be to praise rather than to blame. Thank You for showing me Your purposes in my times of pain.

FINDING STRENGTH IN GOD

COLOSSIANS 1:10–12

walk worthy of the Lord, fully pleasing to Him, bearing fruit in every good work and growing in the knowledge of God. May you be strengthened with all power, according to His glorious might, to produce full endurance and patience with joy, as you give thanks to the Father, who has enabled you to share in the saints' inheritance in the light.

Nothing helps more than finding strength in our God. We can't count on others to give us the encouragement we really need. We'd better be prepared to strengthen ourselves in the Lord. Others can help and be a source of comfort, but this kind of strength comes only from Him.

The most precious and painful times in our Christian experience are times when we are all alone with God. Such times forge an inseparable bond.

I am convinced that sometimes God purposely stays the encouragement of others so we will learn to find it in Him.

PSALM 28:8

The Lord is the strength of His people; He is the saving refuge for His anointed.

The Deeper Question:

How can you learn to find strength in the Lord? What Scriptures have spoken to you when you needed His strength? How has God ministered to you?

_____

_____

_____

_____

_____

_____

_____

_____

_____

_____

_____

_____

_____

_____

_____

_____

_____

Father, I need Your strength. Teach me to walk so closely with You that I draw upon Your power every day and for my every need.

How Victory Is Won

1 Samuel 30:8,17

David asked the LORD, "Am I to pursue this raiding party? Would I overtake it?" "Pursue," He replied, "because you are certain to overtake it and effect the rescue." ... David slaughtered them from twilight until the evening of the next day, and not a man escaped from them except four hundred young men who mounted camels and fled.

Assured victory does not mean an easy win. God told David in advance he would succeed in this rescue, yet we see references to exhaustion, hard work, a non-stop 24-hour battle, and four hundred escapees.

God was absolutely true to His Word. The end was exactly as God had promised, but what we often don't count on is the means. God often gives us a victory that requires blood, sweat, and tears.

Why? Because He is practical. When He can bring about a victory and strengthen and mature us all at the same time, He's likely to do it!

Psalm 18:35

You have given me the shield of Your salvation; Your right hand supports me, and Your humility makes me great.

THE DEEPER QUESTION:

what growth has come in your character as a result of the battles God has brought you through? why are victories that occur in you more important than the victories won through you?

_____

_____

_____

_____

_____

_____

_____

_____

_____

_____

_____

_____

_____

_____

_____

_____

Father God, teach me that what comes out of a battle isn't nearly as important as who comes out of a battle. Work Your victories in me rather than just through me.

THE END OF AN ERA

DEUTERONOMY 11:22-24

"If you truly keep this entire command which I am giving you to follow, by loving the LORD your God, by walking in all His ways and by holding fast to Him, then the LORD will dispossess all these nations before you, and you will dispossess nations greater and stronger than you. Every place on which your foot treads will be yours."

God said He would drive out the other nations before Israel but only if they would "truly keep" all His commands. They didn't. So now, He wouldn't.

As the ghostly Samuel had predicted, Saul saw Israel defeated and his own sons killed. "They killed his sons Jonathan, Abinadab, and Malchi-shua. The fighting became heavy around Saul; the archers hit him, and he was critically wounded" (1 Sam. 31:2-3).

This passage is especially difficult because we feel we've come to know the people who perished. My heart aches at their difficult end.

1 SAMUEL 31:5

when his armor-bearer saw that Saul was dead, he also fell upon his own sword and died with him.

THE DEEPER QUESTION:

How mindful are you of the fleeting nature of time? What are you doing to share Christ with the Souls in your world? What creative methods might you use?

Lord, I know judgment is coming. Give me an urgency to share Christ while I still have the opportunity, and give me wisdom to know how to share it most effectively.

THE DEBT OF LOVE

1 SAMUEL 11:9,11

"Say this to the people of Jabesh-gilead: 'Salvation will be yours tomorrow by the time the sun is hot.' "So the messengers went and told the men of Jabesh, and they rejoiced.... The following day Saul put the men in three groups.... The troops entered into the midst of the camp and struck Ammon until the heat of the day.

Sometimes the worst of events bring out the best in people. When the men of Jabesh Gilead heard of the death of Saul, they remembered how he had saved them so many years before. So they traveled all night and risked their lives to retrieve and bury the bodies.

The men of Jabesh Gilead performed a brave and loving act. They could have ended up impaled right beside the bodies they came to rescue.

I am encouraged to think that after 42 years, the people of the village never forgot their debt of gratitude to a young king who started well.

1 SAMUEL 31:13

They took their bones and buried them under the Tamarisk in Jabesh and fasted seven days.

THE DEEPER QUESTION:

Owe somebody a favor? Do you need to repay it before you stand with them under the shade of a tamarisk tree? What can you do when you are tempted to be disloyal?

Father, build my character so that I may be an example of Your faithfulness. May my memories of kindness be long and of offenses be short.

A Time to Grieve

2 Samuel 1:17,23,26

David sang this lament. . . . "In life, Saul and Jonathan were beloved and delightful; in death, they were inseparable. They were swifter than eagles, stronger than lions. . . . I am so distressed over you, my brother Jonathan. You were such a delight to me. Your love for me was more wonderful than the love of women."

David poured out his love for Jonathan and (in spite of all the years the mad king's jealousy had cost him) for Saul. He wrote his grief in the form of a lament.

David called his friend's love "wonderful." He distinguished the sacrificial nature of this friendship from anything else anyone had ever demonstrated to him.

So determined had Jonathan been for David to be king—a position which Jonathan stood to inherit—that Jonathan committed his entire life to that end. How differently David wished it had all happened.

Psalm 88:9

My eyes are darkened by my misery. Every day I call to You, LORD; I have spread out my hands to You.

THE DEEPER QUESTION:

How does deep grief feel to you? How have you learned to pour out your grief? How does grief change your relationship with God? Can you grow through grief?

_____

_____

_____

_____

_____

_____

_____

_____

_____

_____

_____

_____

_____

_____

_____

_____

_____

Lord Jesus, You have experienced all we face in life. Walk with me through my times of grief, and draw me into a more intimate walk with You.

IN THE COURSE OF TIME

2 SAMUEL 2:1-2,4

After this, David asked the LORD, "Should I go up to one of the towns of Judah?" "Go up," the LORD said to him. Then David said, "Where should I go?" "To Hebron," the LORD replied. So David went up there.... Then the men of Judah came and anointed David there as king over the house of Judah.

Some things just take the course of time. Nothing else works.

You can bet some lonely hours filled David's "course of time." Some tears. Some regrets. Some endless replays. Some anger. Some confusion. But it did finally pass. Not the ache, but the pain. Blessedly, thankfully. In the course of time.

David had waited at least 15 years for the fulfillment of the kingly promise made through Samuel. Now after a period of mourning for Saul and Jonathan, David was finally ready to become the king of Judah—and eventually of all Israel.

EXODUS 9:5-6

The LORD set a time, saying, "Tomorrow the LORD will do this thing in the land." So the LORD did this thing the next day.

THE DEEPER QUESTION:

what have you learned about the Lord's use of time? How do you react to the statement that God uses time as a tool in His hand? Have you learned that waiting is an integral part of serving Christ?

_____

_____

_____

_____

_____

_____

_____

_____

_____

_____

_____

_____

_____

_____

_____

Christ, You are the Lord not only of eternity but of today. Teach me to trust You to bring things to me in their proper time—at just the right moment.

INQUIRING OF THE LORD

2 SAMUEL 2:1-4

David asked the LORD, "Should I go up to one of the towns of Judah?" "Go up," the LORD said to him. Then David asked, "Where should I go?" "To Hebron," the LORD replied. So David went up . . . and they dwelt in the towns of Hebron. Then the men of Judah came and anointed David there as king over the house of Judah.

I know this is the same Scripture as the page before, but this second point is worth making: David kept asking until he had a specific answer from God. He did not want general directions. He wanted to know God's exact will for his life. He wasn't interested in simply getting to the throne. He wanted to get to the throne God's way.

At times I have asked God's direction, then assumed my first hunch was His will for my life. I'm learning to be more patient and allow God to be more specific if He wishes. No matter how long we may wait for direction, we are wise to ask before we advance.

EXODUS 33:15

"If Your presence does not lead, do not take us out of this place."

THE DEEPER QUESTION:

Can you identify times when you proceeded in a certain direction because of a hunch rather than the confirmed will of God? What have you learned from the experience?

_____

_____

_____

_____

_____

_____

_____

_____

_____

_____

_____

_____

_____

_____

_____

_____

_____

Father, teach me to wait on You until you confirm Your will. Then give me the courage to follow wherever You lead.

THE GOD WHO SPEAKS, PART I

PSALM 119:18,98-100

uncover my eyes, that I may see the wonderful things to be found in Your law. . . . Your commandment makes me wiser than my enemies, for it is with me forever. I have more insight than all my teachers, for Your testimonies are my meditaiton. I understand more than the elders, for I have kept Your precepts.

We have something that those who lived during the Old Testament did not have: His written and completed Word. God will speak specifically to us through Scripture if we learn how to listen.

God has taught me a method that may take time but always works. It consists of four general steps. Let's consider the first two now, and the rest tomorrow. First, I acknowledge my specific needs for direction, whatever I'm needing that day. I almost always write my question in a journal—like this one—so that I can keep a record of God's activity. Then, second, I continue to pray daily and study His Word.

PSALM 119:14

I rejoice in the way of Your testimonies as much as in all kinds of wealth.

THE DEEPER QUESTION:

Which is more important to you: to have the answer to your question or to have fellowship with God? How has seeking God's will led you to increased intimacy with God?

_____

_____

_____

_____

_____

_____

_____

_____

_____

_____

_____

_____

_____

_____

_____

_____

Father, teach me to hunger and thirst after You. Guide me to Your will, but more importantly, lead me to Your heart.

THE GOD WHO SPEAKS, PART II

PSALM 119:26-27,32,45

I recounted my ways, and You answered my prayer; teach me Your statutes. Make me understand the way of Your precepts, that I might meditate on Your wonders.... I run the way of Your commandments, for You set my heart free ... that I might walk about in freedom, for I have sought out Your precepts.

Back to my four-part method for hearing God in the Scripture. After I specifically acknowledge my need for God's guidance and continue in prayer and study, I ask Him to help me recognize His answer. I resist reading into my situation everything God's Word says. I specifically ask Him to confirm with His Word *and* His Spirit what He desires to apply to my life.

One or two weeks later I might be studying a particular passage of Scripture, and His Holy Spirit will almost say, "Look, Beth, that's it!" But, fourth, if I have any doubt, I ask Him for confirmation.

PSALM 5:8

Lead me in Your righteousness, LORD, because of my adversaries; make Your way smooth in front of me.

THE DEEPER QUESTION:

How has God directed your path in the past? What wrong turns have you made along the way? Can you see more clearly now? Are you willing to take the time to seek Him until you know Him?

_____

_____

_____

_____

_____

_____

_____

_____

_____

_____

_____

_____

_____

_____

_____

_____

_____

Lord, I want to follow closely in Your footsteps. Teach me when to wait, how to listen, and when to move forward in obedience.

A Legacy of Jealousy

2 Samuel 3:1,7

The war between the house of Saul and the house of David was long and drawn out, with David steadily growing stronger and the house of Saul weaker. . . . Now Saul had a concubine whose name was Rizpah, daughter of Aiah. Ishbosheth said to Abner: "Why did you have sex with my father's concubine?"

David was anointed king over Judah, but the other tribes followed Saul's son Ish-bosheth. The result was a civil war where the forces of David slowly wore down the house of Saul.

In the life of Ish-bosheth we see a fact sadly reflective of human life. Through their behavior, parents teach their children to repeat the family sins. Just as jealousy had proved Saul's undoing, now his son became jealous and suspicious of someone who had been on his side.

What better reason to stay diligent about asking God for help with our weaknesses than to stop the flow of certain sins to our children.

Psalm 78:4

We must not hide them from their descendants; to a coming generation we must recount the praises of the LORD.

THE DEEPER QUESTION:

With what family character traits have you had to struggle? Are the ongoing difficulties of jealousy, anger, or a critical spirit among your inheritances? What are you passing to the next generation?

_____

_____

_____

_____

_____

_____

_____

_____

_____

_____

_____

_____

_____

_____

_____

_____

Father, sometimes I hear the words of my parents come from my own mouth. Teach me to honor the positive parts of my legacy but to change those parts that are less than godly.

BLINDED BY BLOODLINES

2 SAMUEL 3:26-27

When he left David's presence, Joab sent messengers after Abner. They brought him back from the pool of Sirah, but David was unaware of it. When Abner returned to Hebron, Joab pulled him inside the gateway, as if to speak to him privately, and there Joab stabbed him in the stomach. So Abner died in revenge for the death of Asahel, Joab's brother.

Joab, the general of David's army, was a vengeful and murderous man, but time after time David allowed Joab's actions to go unpunished.

We would wonder why David put up with Joab's evil but for two facts. First, we learn in 1 Chronicles 2:13-17 that Joab was David's nephew. Second, David doubtless felt that he owed Joab loyalty because they had weathered the fugitive years together.

Sometimes justice is more important than loyalty or lineage. In David's life, the lines had begun to blur.

2 SAMUEL 3:38

The king said to his soldiers, "Don't you know that today a great prince in Israel has fallen?"

THE DEEPER QUESTION:

In what situations are you willing to compromise justice? Do your friendships or family ties sometimes cloud your judgment? What always happens when you fail to deal with wrong behavior?

Lord, I sometimes find it easy—like David—to take the path of least resistance. Give me the courage to make difficult decisions whenever necessary.

THIS MUCH WE KNOW

2 SAMUEL 5:1-3

All the tribes of Israel came to David in Hebron and said: "Look, we are your flesh and blood. . . . The LORD said to you, 'You will shepherd my people Israel.'" . . . when all the elders of Israel came to the king at Hebron, King David made a covenant with them in Hebron before the LORD. So they anointed David as king over Israel.

When God handed over the most fortified city in all Israel to David and placed favor in the heart of the king of Tyre toward him, David knew the Lord had established him!

You may be going through a confusing time. You may not know how God is going to use a situation in your life or why certain things have happened to you. But you can be encouraged and strengthened by recalling what you know about God in the midst of uncertainties.

In confusing times, recounting what we do know refreshes us. You may never know why or how, but you can know God will be faithful.

2 SAMUEL 5:12

David knew the LORD had established him as king over all Israel and had exalted his kingdom for the sake of His people Israel.

THE DEEPER QUESTION:

What do you know about God that can sustain you during times of uncertainty? How has He sustained you in the past? If you cannot celebrate your circumstances, celebrate Him!

_____

_____

_____

_____

_____

_____

_____

_____

_____

_____

_____

_____

_____

_____

_____

_____

_____

_____

_____

Lord, I have known many times of uncertainty and questions. Remind me that though I may never know why or how, I can always know who is faithful.

HANDS TRAINED FOR WAR

PSALM 18:31-34

who is God besides the LORD? And who is a rock except our God? The God who equips me with strength, and makes my way blameless, who makes my feet like those of a doe, and makes me stand firmly on my high places, who trains my hands for war; my arms can bend a bow of bronze.

David had come so far, yet he was back where he started.

The hand that wrapped around his weapon as he waited for God's signal to overcome the Philistines looked far different from the hand that had searched for a smooth stone many years before. Now he stood against them once more.

To a man on the run, the Philistines had been a temporary refuge. They had taken advantage of his homeless estate by enjoying his strength. To a king on his rightful throne, however, they were clearly an enemy once more. And he knew God—again—would give him success.

REVELATION 19:11

There was a white horse! Its rider is called Faithful and True, and in righteousness He judges and makes war.

THE DEEPER QUESTION:

What battles has the Lord led you through? What kinds of battles are you facing today? Why do you suppose this Christian walk must always involve an element of warfare?

_____

_____

_____

_____

_____

_____

_____

_____

_____

_____

_____

_____

_____

_____

_____

_____

_____

_____

_____

_____

_____

_____

Lord Jesus, I see in Scripture and in my life that to follow You means to be a soldier. Train me and use me to glorify my King.

A Name for Every Need

Psalm 18:1–2,6

*I love you, LORD, my strength. The LORD is
my rock, my fortress, and my deliverer; He
is my God, my rock, in whom I seek refuge;
He is my shield and the horn of my salvation, my stronghold. . . . In my distress, I
called to the LORD; to my God I cried for help.
He heard my voice from His temple; my cry
to Him for help entered His ears.*

David called God by many names: my Rock, my loving God, my
fortress, my stronghold, my deliverer, my shield, my refuge, the one
who trains my hands and who subdues peoples under me. For all of
David's needs, his God had a name.

We, too, can know God by a name for every need. David knew without a doubt that God had given him victory and subdued the people
under his leadership. He still didn't know why. He simply knew Who.

The names David called his God fell from the lips of experience, from
things he knew.

Psalm 23:1–2

*The LORD is my shepherd; I lack nothing.
He makes me lie down in green pastures.
He leads me beside calm waters.*

THE DEEPER QUESTION:

what do you know of God from experience? What names for Himself has He given you through those experiences? Are you talking with Him through all of your struggles?

_____

_____

_____

_____

_____

_____

_____

_____

_____

_____

_____

_____

_____

_____

Father, I do not want to have a second-hand relationship with You. Lead me to treasure my experiences with You and to save them in my heart.

Serious Obedience

2 Samuel 6:2-3

David got up and went with all his troops to bring up from Baale-judah the ark of God.... They set the ark of God on a new cart and brought it from the house of Abinadab, which was on the hill. Uzzah and Ahio, sons of Abinadab, were guiding the new cart.

God masterfully designed the transportation of His glory to literally rest on the shoulders of His revering priests, not on the backs of beasts.

David's actions in transporting the ark not only disregarded the Lord's instructions, they included a greater insult. When the Philistines captured the ark, God caused them seven months of devastation. To rid themselves of the troublesome ark, the Philistines loaded it on a cart pulled by two cows.

Now David imitated the actions of the Philistines rather than obey the commands of God.

Deuteronomy 17:18

When he is installed as king, he must write a copy of this law for himself on a scroll.

THE DEEPER QUESTION:

How seriously do you take obedience to God? Do you ever consider obedience in small details to be optional? How does your modeling affect the attitudes of others regarding obedience to God?

_____

_____

_____

_____

_____

_____

_____

_____

_____

_____

_____

_____

_____

_____

_____

_____

_____

_____

_____

_____

_____

Lord, build in me a deep reverence for Your commands. Never let me develop a cavalier attitude toward my obedience to You.

From Dancing to Mourning

2 Samuel 6:5-7

David and all the house of Israel were playing music before the LORD. . . . When they came to the threshing floor of Nacon, Uzzah stretched out his hand to grab the ark of God, because the oxen stumbled. The anger of the LORD blazed against Uzzah, and God struck him there because of his impudence, and he died there alongside the ark of God.

Imagine becoming emotionally geared for a great celebration of bringing the ark of God to Jerusalem, only to greet disaster instead.

Uzzah's death would have been shocking under the most somber of circumstances, but can you imagine the shock in the midst of such celebration? David must have felt like he jumped off an emotional cliff.

Surely all of us have experienced an unexpected, uninvited emotional dive. Devastation is always heartbreaking. Devastation that should have been celebration is almost more than we can take.

1 Peter 1:6

You rejoice in this; however, now for a short time, if it is necessary, you may be distressed by various trials.

THE DEEPER QUESTION:

Have you ever experienced loss when you expected joy? How can you support others in such times? What kinds of comments are unhelpful at such times?

_____

_____

_____

_____

_____

_____

_____

_____

_____

_____

_____

_____

_____

_____

_____

_____

_____

_____

_____

_____

_____

Lord, sometimes my expectations set me up for great disappointment. Teach me to delight myself in You even when circumstances seem against all that I desire.

ANGRY AND AFRAID

2 SAMUEL 6:8-10

David was angry because the LORD's anger had broken forth against Uzzah. . . . David feared the LORD on that day and said, "How can the ark of the LORD come to me?" So David was reluctant to move the ark of the LORD to the city of David. Instead, he diverted it to the house of Obed-edom the Gittite.

After God killed Uzzah, David felt two powerful emotions: anger and fear. Note that he felt anger and fear toward God, yet Scripture calls him "a man after God's own heart."

I think one reason David remained a man after God's own heart was his unwillingness to turn from God, even when he felt negative emotions. David allowed his anger and fear to motivate him to seek more insight into the heart of God.

We need to follow David's example by allowing our questions and confusion to motivate us to seek God.

1 THESSALONIANS 3:7

In all our distress and persecution, we were encouraged about you through your faith.

THE DEEPER QUESTION:

How do you react when you feel angry or afraid of God? Do you allow yourself to recognize these emotions? Why or why not? How can fear be a part of a healthy attitude toward God?

_____

_____

_____

_____

_____

_____

_____

_____

_____

_____

_____

_____

_____

_____

_____

_____

Almighty God, I confess that I sometimes want to replace You with a tamer god whom I can manage. Don't let me settle for anything less than an authentic relationship with You.

WORSHIP WITH ABANDON

2 SAMUEL 6:12-15

*David went and brought up the ark of God.
... when those carrying the ark of the LORD
had advanced six steps, he sacrificed an ox
and a fattened steer. Now David was dancing
with all his might before the LORD, girded
with a linen ephod, as he and all the house of
Israel were bringing up the ark of the LORD
with shouts and the sound of the trumpet.*

Worship with abandon is an intimate experience. We see David almost oblivious to everyone around him, totally liberated in the spirit, dancing through the streets of Jerusalem "with all his might."

Oh, I love this scene! Centuries later, a group of disciples were stunned when Mary of Bethany poured the fragrance of abandoned worship on Christ's feet (John 12:1-8).

But completely abandoned worship is often misunderstood. David's wife, Michal, saw David dancing through the streets of Jerusalem, and she burned with jealousy. Can you worship when it costs you?

ZEPHANIAH 2:11

*The nations on every shore will bow down to
Him, each from its own place.*

THE DEEPER QUESTION:

What causes you to hold back from completely abandoned worship? How does it feel to abandon self in the worship of God? How does it feel to be misunderstood by others?

_____

_____

_____

_____

_____

_____

_____

_____

_____

_____

_____

_____

_____

_____

_____

_____

Precious Christ, whether or not my family does, whether or not my friends do, whether or not my nation does, help me to celebrate before the Lord!

LEARNING TO WAIL

PSALM 30:5,11-12

Though we spend a moment in His anger, we will have a lifetime in His favor. Weeping may spend the evening, but in the morning will come a shout for joy. . . . You have turned my mourning into dancing; You have removed my sackcloth and wrapped me in joy, so that my spirit will sing praise to You and not be silent. O LORD my God, I will praise You forever.

I'm not sure we'll ever be released to fully "dance" before the Lord until we've learned to wail.

Like David, you may be angry at God for taking someone's life you cared for deeply. I urge you to be like David, willing to wait, to study, to hear God's Word, and to approach Him again.

God is not harsh; He is holy. He is not selfish; He is sovereign. He is not unfeeling; He is all-knowing.

Like David, we need to come to know Him and respect Him and—like David—we will love Him more.

JEREMIAH 20:7

You tried to persuade me, LORD, and I was persuaded; You have taken hold of me and have prevailed.

THE DEEPER QUESTION:

Does God permit you to wail as well as to dance? Which emotions are okay, and which are off limits? In your experience, how has wailing been a doorway to intimacy with God?

_____

_____

_____

_____

_____

_____

_____

_____

_____

_____

_____

_____

_____

_____

_____

_____

_____

Father, I want our relationship to be real rather than religious. Teach me to know, respect, love, and honor You in all that I do today.

THE STUFF OF KINGS

2 SAMUEL 7:1-3

When the king was living in his palace and the LORD had granted him rest on every side from all his enemies, the king said to Nathan the prophet, "Look! I'm living in a cedar palace, but the ark of God remains inside curtains." Nathan responded to the king, "Go and do all that is in your heart, for the LORD is with you."

We've all experienced a sudden bout of sober realization, times when we were horror struck by our own audacity. This was one of those times in the life of David.

Life was calm. Enemies were subdued. Perhaps he was taking a load off, perched on his throne, when suddenly his eyes were unveiled to the splendor around him. He looked around and thought, "What's wrong with this picture?"

Several virtues could be noted in David's sudden reaction to his surroundings. But one—humility—is a quality not found in many kings.

MATTHEW 19:21

"Go, sell your belongings and give to the poor, and you will have treasure in heaven. Then come, follow Me."

THE DEEPER QUESTION:

How have you encountered your own audacity? Have you been struck by the realization of your riches? of your pride? How does God communicate with you at such times?

_____

_____

_____

_____

_____

_____

_____

_____

_____

_____

_____

_____

_____

_____

_____

_____

_____

_____

_____

_____

Father, I see that You have given me so much compared to the needs of the world. Guide me to use in Your service what You have given.

WANTING WHAT'S BEST

2 SAMUEL 7:11-13

"The LORD himself will make a dynasty for you. When your days end and you rest with your fathers, I will raise up your descendant after you, who will come from your body, and I will establish his kingdom. He will build a temple for My name, and I will establish the throne of his kingdom forever."

God chose to have His temple built during a reign not characterized by David's warfare but by Solomon's peace.

I am touched by the mercy of God toward His beloved David. He did not snatch the privilege from him in judgment. Rather, He allowed David's son to receive the honor.

What could be better than being appointed to do a marvelous task for God? For me, it would be for my child to do a marvelous task for God! I would happily forfeit participation in the great things of God for my children to inherit the opportunity!

PROVERBS 3:1-2

Don't forget my teaching, but let your heart guard my commands, for more days and years of life and peace they will add to you.

THE DEEPER QUESTION:

What do you wish for your children or for children you know? How are you praying for them? How is desiring the best for children different than forcing them into a parent's mold?

_____

_____

_____

_____

_____

_____

_____

_____

_____

_____

_____

_____

_____

_____

_____

Father, as much as I desire to be used, it means even more to watch You use those I love. Grant that I may influence them to serve You.

THINK ON IT AWHILE

2 SAMUEL 7:4-5,7

That night the word of the LORD came to Nathan: "Go and say to my servant David, 'This is what the LORD says: Are you the one to build a house for Me to dwell in? ... Have I ever asked anyone from the tribes of Israel whom I commanded to shepherd My people Israel, "Why haven't you built Me a house of cedar?"'"

God taught both the king and his prophet a gentle lesson on making assumptions. He had something to say to each man. Perhaps we would be wise to heed as well.

To David, God was saying, "Don't assume that every bright and noble idea in a godly man's mind is of Me." Good ideas and God's ideas are often completely different.

And to Nathan, God was saying, "Don't assume that a leader I have chosen is always right." The Lord can be *with* a man, but that man can make a decision *without* God.

NUMBERS 9:8

Moses said to them, "Stand here so that I may hear what the LORD commands concerning you."

The Deeper Question:

Have you assumed that an idea from a Christian leader was just automatically from God? How can you take more seriously your own responsibility to seek God's will?

_____

_____

_____

_____

_____

_____

_____

_____

_____

_____

_____

_____

_____

_____

_____

_____

_____

_____

Lord, I sometimes jump to conclusions about Your will. Teach me to wait on You. I want to value Your presence far more than the jobs You give me to do.

HE'S HERE, WHEREVER YOU ARE

2 SAMUEL 7:6-7

"I've not dwelt in a building from the time I brought the Israelites up from Egypt till this day. Instead, I've been moving about in a tent as My dwelling. In all My wanderings among the Israelites, have I ever asked anyone from the tribes of Israel whom I commanded to shepherd My people Israel, 'why haven't you built Me a house of cedar?'"

Building on the same passage and theme as yesterday's, we see that in the rebuke to Nathan, God seems to be saying, "As long as my people are on the move, I'm on the move! You can't tie me down as long as my people are mobile!"

Isn't He wonderful? The tent to which God was referring was the Old Testament tabernacle, designed by God to move with the people! That's God's way. You can't leave home without Him.

The New Testament says it this way: "The Word became flesh and took up residence among us" (John 1:14).

REVELATION 7:15-16

The One seated on the throne will shelter them: no longer will they hunger; no longer will they thirst.

The Deeper Question:

What does the mobility of God mean to you? How does His traveling presence encourage you? How does it challenge your behavior and keep you aware of His watchful eye?

Lord Jesus, I am amazed that You have chosen to pitch Your tent in me. Remind me today that You are present in every circumstance.

God Does Great Work

2 Samuel 7:11-13

"The LORD himself will make a dynasty for you. When your days end and you rest with your fathers, I will raise up your descendant after you, who will come from your body, and I will establish his kingdom. He will build a temple for My name, and I will establish the throne of his kingdom forever."

We looked at this passage earlier in reference to the satisfaction of seeing God use our children in His plan. But you can also look at this moment another way.

Allow me to paraphrase: "David, you won't build a house for Me. I'm going to build a house for you!" What overwhelming words! We want to do so many things for God, then they suddenly pale in comparison to the realization of all He wants to do for us!

Romans 8:32 says, "He did not even spare His own Son, but offered Him up for us all; how will He not also with Him grant us everything?"

2 Corinthians 5:1

We have a building from God, a house not made with hands, eternal in the heavens.

The Deeper Question:

Why do people naturally seem to prefer works rather than grace? How would you feel in David's place when God promised to build him a house forever?

_____

_____

_____

_____

_____

_____

_____

_____

_____

_____

_____

_____

_____

_____

_____

_____

_____

_____

_____

_____

_____

Lord Jesus, thank You for Your grace. I am so grateful that my life depends on Your faithfulness rather than my performance.

COMPULSORY PRAISE

2 SAMUEL 7:18-20

"Who am I, Lord GOD, and who is my family, that You have brought me this far? Yet, even this was insignificant in Your sight, Lord GOD, for You have also spoken concerning the dynasty of Your servant in the distant future. And this is Your ordinance concerning mankind, O Lord GOD! What more can David say to you?"

Have you ever been so overwhelmed with both the person of God and His actions that you simply had to praise Him?

Imagine for a moment the emotions coursing through David. After all his years of struggle, he finds himself seated on the throne in Jerusalem with rest from all his enemies. Now Nathan the prophet delivers the message that God will bless not only David, but his children.

He must have been overwhelmed. No wonder he "went in and sat before the Lord" (2 Samuel 7:18a) and poured out his heart. Genuine gratitude brings it out of you.

1 CORINTHIANS 15:9-10

I am the least of the apostles, unworthy to be called an apostle. . . . But by God's grace I am what I am.

THE DEEPER QUESTION:

What blessings of God have most overwhelmed you? How have you felt when you recognized what God had done for you? How can you make gratitude a primary characteristic of your life?

O Lord God, You have made the heavens and the earth by Your great power. Thank You for using that power in my life.

SITTING IN HIS PRESENCE

2 SAMUEL 7:21,25-26

"For the sake of Your word and according to Your will, You have bestowed all this honor to let Your servant know. . . . And now, Lord GOD, keep forever the promise You have made concerning Your servant and his dynasty, and do as You have promised, so that Your name may be magnified forever."

Have you experienced a time when you received an answer from God, and you wanted to run as fast as you could and sit before Him? When those moments occur, you can't even explain how you feel. Your can only go and sit before Him.

When I am overwhelmed by something God has done for me or said to me, I often find that I have to sit a moment and wait for my heart to write words on my lips. Sometimes I weep for a while before I can begin to speak.

God is oh so incredibly good.

ROMANS 11:33

Oh, the depth of the riches both of the wisdom and the knowledge of God!

THE DEEPER QUESTION:

Where is your personal place to sit before the Lord? What have been your most significant times of sitting before God in the past year? What can you do to establish such times?

O Sovereign Lord, who am I, and what is my family, that You have brought me this far? I praise You for raising me up to sit in heavenly places with You.

CRIPPLED IN BOTH FEET

2 SAMUEL 9:3,7

"Is there still anyone belonging to Saul's family to whom I may show God's faithful love?" . . . "There is still a son of Jonathan who is crippled in both feet." . . . David said to him, "Don't be afraid, because I intend to show you faithful love for the sake of Jonathan your father. I will restore all the fields of your grandfather Saul to you."

David looked around at the kingdom and thought of the man who first planned to share it. He missed Jonathan, and in spite of all Saul did, I believe he still loved Saul.

You hear David's loneliness at the top when he says, "Is there still anyone belonging to Saul's family to whom I may show God's faithful love?"

All was momentarily quiet and peaceful, and he missed his best friend. God had fulfilled Jonathan's wish and given David everything, but he wasn't there to share it with him. Some things hurt for life.

2 SAMUEL 9:8

Mephibosheth prostrated himself and said, "What is your servant that you should have regard for a dead dog like me?"

THE DEEPER QUESTION:

With whom in this story do you identify? With David's loneliness? With Methphibosheth's feelings of alienation? In what sense have you been "crippled in both feet"?

_____

_____

_____

_____

_____

_____

_____

_____

_____

_____

_____

_____

_____

_____

_____

_____

_____

_____

_____

Father, thank You so much for showing Your love for Your son Jesus to a "dead dog like me." You shower me with Your goodness and mercy.

ROOM AT THE TABLE

2 SAMUEL 9:9,11,13

The king summoned Zibah, Saul's servant, and instructed him, "All that belonged to Saul and all his household I've entrusted to the grandson of your master."... So Mephibosheth ate at the table just like the sons of the king.... Mephibosheth lived in Jerusalem, since he always ate at the king's table. He was crippled in both feet.

David had a desire for another son. He came before Mephibosheth to make him a son. He was family—invited to sit at the king's table to partake of his fellowship as one of his own!

Imagine the sight when he first limped to the table set with sumptuous delights, surrounded by festive activity, and sat down, resting his crippled legs at the king's table.

Hallelujah! We are like Mephibosheth! No matter how many sons the Father has, He still wants more to conform into the image of His first and only begotten.

1 JOHN 3:1

Look at how great a love the Father has given us, that we should be called God's children. And we are!

THE DEEPER QUESTION:

When did you first realize that God wanted you as his child? How did you feel then? How do you feel today about God's desire for you at His table?

_____

_____

_____

_____

_____

_____

_____

_____

_____

_____

_____

_____

_____

_____

_____

_____

I praise You, my shame destroyer—the lover of the lame. I will marvel through the ages that You make room at Your table for me. I love You so much.

Up on the Rooftop

2 Samuel 11:1-2,4

In the spring, when kings go to war, David sent Joab with his officers and all the Israelite army . . . but David remained at Jerusalem. One evening, David got up from his bed and walked about on the roof of the palace. From the roof, he saw a woman bathing. The woman was very beautiful. . . . Then David sent messengers to get her.

David had grown dangerously accustomed to having all he wanted. The outcome of his eroding self-control tumbled him headlong into the pit of sin.

So, disregarding common decency, when he saw the beautiful wife of one of his soldiers bathing, he sent for her. They committed adultery, and she became pregnant.

We, too, could be persons of character and integrity, and without apparent warning, destroy our ministries and ourselves through the choice to gratify our sudden lusts.

Proverbs 6:32

whoever commits adultery with a woman is absolutely senseless; he destroys his life when he does it.

The Deeper Question:

How does avoiding responsibility open us up to more temptation? Have you thought you were safe from choosing to sin? How have you found yourself choosing a sin you thought you would never commit?

_____

_____

_____

_____

_____

_____

_____

_____

_____

_____

_____

_____

_____

_____

_____

Lord, I know I can fall like David before sin's onslaught. Keep me walking close to You today so I do not become vulnerable to the destructive temptations of the evil one.

SIN ON TOP OF SIN

2 SAMUEL 11:11,14-15

Uriah answered David: ... The soldiers of my lord are camping in the open field. How can I go to my house to eat and drink and lie with my wife? As you live and as your soul lives, I'll not do such a thing!" ... David wrote a letter to Joab. ... "Put Uriah in the front of the fiercest fighting, and then withdraw from him so that he may be struck down and die."

The Scripture gives no hint that Uriah recognized the dishonesty of his king. To the contrary, his honor spoiled David's plan. Uriah refused to go home to his wife when his comrades were in the field.

This act of honor put David on the spot. At this point, he had the opportunity to either confess his sin or to cover it with still more evil. He foolishly chose the latter.

In one of the great betrayals of history, David wrote orders to have Uriah killed—even giving them to Uriah to deliver. Thus Bathsheba's husband trustingly carried his own death warrant to his executioner.

PROVERBS 28:13

Whoever covers over his own offenses will not prosper, but anyone who confesses and abandons them will find compassion.

THE DEEPER QUESTION:

why do you think David didn't stop and repent? Consider the answer from a personal standpoint, "why have I not at times stopped and repented in the earlier stages of sin?"

Father, I sometimes lack the courage to ask forgiveness of You or others. Fear can paralyze me. Train me in the fine art of confession.

BROKEN SILENCE

PSALM 32:3-5

when I kept silent, my body wasted away with my groaning all day long. For day and night Your hand lay heavily upon me; my strength was sapped as in the dry heat of summer. I acknowledged to You my sin, and I did not try to hide my guilt. When I said, "I will confess my offenses to the LORD," You took away the guilt of my sin.

I believe Psalm 32 describes a malady we might call sin-sickness.

During periods when I refused to repent of sin in my life, I felt sapped of strength and sick all over. I groaned in my sin. Thankfully, the seasons of my sin and rebellion were the most miserable periods of my life, worse than any uninvited suffering I've ever experienced. I needed it to hurt, so that I would never choose to go there again.

God graciously forgave me once I repented, and He forgot my sin, but I am thankful He did not allow me to forget. We need this grieving process. We need to know how deeply we have offended God.

2 SAMUEL 12:5,7

David was very angry at the man. . . . Then Nathan said to David, "You are the man!"

THE DEEPER QUESTION:

How does unrepented sin affect you? How do you feel when you finally acknowledge a long-denied or hidden sin? Why do you suppose we so resist the relief of forgiveness?

_____

_____

_____

_____

_____

_____

_____

_____

_____

_____

_____

_____

_____

_____

_____

Lord Jesus, thank You for bearing the unimaginable weight of all my sin on Your cross. Teach me to admit it when I sin, and give me the strength to turn from it.

THE BALM OF FORGIVENESS

PSALM 51:1-2,7-8

Be gracious to me, O God, according to Your faithful love. According to the abundance of Your compassion, wipe away my offenses. wash me thoroughly of my guilt, and cleanse me of my sin.... Purify me with hyssop that I may be clean; wash me that I may be whiter than snow. Let me hear joy and happiness, that the bones You have crushed may rejoice.

Somewhere between confronting sin and restoring fellowship must come the bridge between those two vital works—contrite confession. In Psalm 51 we have the blueprint for this bridge of confession, fresh from the heart of a grieving king.

Don't miss the important emphasis in this statement: "Wash me thoroughly of my guilt"—all of it. What a wonderful word—*all!* The mercy of God is enough to cover all our sins.

Few things in life are as fresh and thrilling to me as that moment when I know God has heard my repentant cry and I am completely clean.

MICAH 7:18

who is a God like You, who bears away guilt, who passes over rebellion for the remnant of His inheritance?

THE DEEPER QUESTION:

Are you able to accept that all your confessed and rejected sins have been completely forgiven? If not, what do you think holds you back from accepting God's complete forgiveness?

Thank You, merciful God, for the words You placed in the heart and on the pen of a broken king. Thank You most of all for forgiveness. May I never be able to resist.

PASSIVE PARENTING

2 SAMUEL 13:20-21;15:10

Tamar lived desolate in the house of her brother Absalom. When King David heard about all these things, he was very angry.... Then Absalom sent scouts throughout the tribes of Israel saying, "When you hear the sound of the trumpet, say, 'Absalom has become king in Hebron!'"

Absalom became deeply alienated from his father when his brother Amnon had raped Tamar, and David had done nothing. David got *mad*, but he never took his rightful place of authority over his family.

The results of David's passive parenting were devastating. Absalom tried everything he knew—good and bad—to get his father's attention. He even set the fields on fire to get his father to take notice.

Eventually, he became obsessed with vengeance and was determined his father would pay. If he couldn't get his attention, he would take his throne.

PROVERBS 27:5-6

Better an open reprimand than concealed love. The wounds of a friend are trustworthy; the kisses of an enemy are abundant.

THE DEEPER QUESTION:

How did your parents deal with problems? Did they confront and solve them? Ignore them? Become angry but do nothing about them? What is your style of dealing with problems? What should it be?

_____

_____

_____

_____

_____

_____

_____

_____

_____

_____

_____

_____

_____

_____

_____

_____

_____

_____

_____

Father, teach me to confront problems with love and grace. Remind me of the bitter fruit that comes from ignoring problems.

SNAP DECISIONS

2 SAMUEL 16:3-4

"Where's your master's son?" the king asked. "Why, he's staying in Jerusalem," Ziba replied to the king, "for he said, 'Today, the house of Israel will restore my father's kingdom to me.'" The king said to Ziba, "All that belongs to Mephibosheth is yours!" "I bow down before you!" Ziba said. "May you look favorably on me, my lord the king!"

Can you ever remember feeling as though someone took advantage of you at a time when you were vulnerable, when personal difficulties were causing you to lack discernment?

Ziba lied about Mephibosheth, David's adopted son. And David's vulnerability caused him to believe the worst. He responded with haste rather than prudence.

We are wise to be careful about the decisions and assumptions we make when we are stressed. At those times, we tend to react rather than respond. We don't make our best decisions when pain is acute.

PROVERBS 1:5

The wise one should listen so that he may increase learning, and the discerning one will acquire guidance.

THE DEEPER QUESTION:

How do you tend to make decisions when under stress? What has past experience taught you about snap decisions? How can you implement the Scripture's teaching to seek wise counsel?

Lord, we humans crucified You through our snap decisions. Teach me wisdom, including the humility to seek godly counsel and to question the opinions of those around me.

Adding Insult to Injury

2 Samuel 16:5-7,11

A man named Shimei son of Gera . . . threw stones at David and all the king's servants. . . . As he cursed, Shimei said, "Get out, get out, you murderer and scoundrel!" . . . David said, "My son, my own flesh and blood, is seeking my life; how much more now this Benjamite! Leave him alone! If he curses, it's because the LORD instructed him."

David might have been saying: "My own beloved son has rejected me. There is nothing anyone can do to injure me any more deeply. Let him go ahead. Maybe I deserve it."

I want to express something to you that I hope you'll receive with your whole heart: We can still cry out to God for help even when we think we're getting what we deserve!

God comes to us even when our pain is self-inflicted. Times of humiliation and persecution do not have to be permanent injuries.

2 Samuel 16:14

The king and all the people with him came to the Jordan exhausted; but they were refreshed there.

THE DEEPER QUESTION:

How can you refresh yourself when you've been down a rocky path? Who has supported you when you were at your low points? How can you support others?

Lord, thank You for supporting me when I have been in the pits and for sending others to support me. Help me be that kind of support to others when they hurt.

Self-Absorbed

2 Samuel 18:14,17

Joab said, "I'm not going to waste time here with you!" He took three javelins in his hand and thrust them into Absalom's heart while he was still alive in the midst of the oak tree. . . . They took Absalom, threw him into a large pit in the forest, and piled a huge mound of stones over him.

The people of Israel often set up stones as a memorial to a significant event—either good or bad. The rocks over the body of Absalom did not just keep wild animals away; they served as a traitor's reminder.

I see great irony in the fact that, as you continue reading into verse 18, you find that Absalom had earlier erected a monument himself—a pillar he intended to immortalize his name for the generations.

These verses demonstrate that Absalom's death as a traitor remains far more memorable than his self-absorbed life. Through bitterness, his heart had become as hard and cold as the pillar he raised.

James 3:16

where envy and selfish ambition exist, there is disorder and every kind of evil.

The Deeper Question:

What characterizes a life as self-absorbed? How do you develop a self-absorbed life? What would you prescribe to treat the disease of self-absorption?

_____

_____

_____

_____

_____

_____

_____

_____

_____

_____

_____

_____

_____

_____

_____

Father, I do not want to be the kind of person who is absorbed with my self, my accomplishments, or my problems. Teach me to center myself on You and to focus on healthy service to others.

STRAIGHT TALK

2 SAMUEL 19:5-6

Joab went to the king's residence and said, "You have shamed your servants today— those who rescued your life, and the lives of your sons and daughters, and the lives of your wives and concubines—by loving those who hate you and hating those who love you. For you have made it clear today that the officers and troops mean nothing to you."

Grief over Absalom was crippling and consuming David. Once again Joab stepped in, this time with some straight talk. He warned that unless David started acting like a king, everyone would desert him.

The next time I suffer a painful loss, remind me not to call someone like Joab for a sympathetic ear. I think a pretty good rule when a friend is grieving is to offer hugs and say little.

Joab may have been thinking as an army commander, looking out for the best interests of his soldiers. But somewhere in his words is the guilt of the man who himself had taken the life of David's son.

ECCLESIASTES 9:17

The calm words of the wise are heeded more than the shouts of one who rules over fools.

THE DEEPER QUESTION:

Has a friend confronted you with hard truth when you didn't want to hear? How difficult is it for you to confront someone? Do you need to work on confrontation skills—or gentleness skills?

Father, thank You for both the people who support in love and those who confront in truth. Teach me to value both and to meet both needs in the lives of my friends.

God's Long Memory

2 Samuel 21:1,3

During David's reign there were three consecutive years of famine. David sought the LORD, and the LORD said, "It comes from Saul and his blood-stained family because he put the Gibeonites to death.". . . David asked the Gibeonites, "What shall I do for you? How can I make atonement so that you may bless the inheritance of the LORD?"

When Israel conquered Palestine, they made an ill-advised treaty with the Gibeonites. Then 300 years later, Saul sought to destroy the Gibeonites.

But God has a long memory. God meant for His people to be good for their word. And He still does.

Surely one reason He expects His people to be good for their word is so that observers might come to believe He is good for His. Israel had to keep her agreement with the Gibeonites even though they should never have entered the agreement.

Ecclesiastes 5:5-6

Better that you do not vow than that you vow and not fulfill it. Do not let your mouth bring guilt upon you.

THE DEEPER QUESTION:

Why do you think God has such a long memory regarding sin? How does punishment for disobedience fit with God's grace? What positive results come from God's righteous punishment of sin?

_____

_____

_____

_____

_____

_____

_____

_____

_____

_____

_____

_____

_____

_____

_____

_____

_____

Father, we so easily reduce You to a heavenly grandfather who only does what we desire. Teach me to see You as You truly are, in all Your holiness and glory.

A Mother's Love

2 Samuel 21:9-10

All seven died at one time. They were put to death in the first days of the barley harvest. Rizpah, daughter of Aiah, set up a sackcloth tent for herself on the rock. From the beginning of harvest until the water poured on them from the sky, she did not allow the birds of the sky to land on them by day or the wild animals at night.

Disasters and times of great loss often provide something else: a demonstration of great love and character. Such was the case for Rizpah, the mother of two of the men killed by the Gibeonites.

As rain drenched her hair, a grieving mother gathered her sackcloth and returned home. The mental image of a mother guarding her sons' bodies from predators was obviously more than David could shake.

The image reawakened old pictures from years past that disturbed him so deeply—the exposed bodies of Saul and his dear friend, Jonathan (1 Samuel 31). True love remains with its beloved to the grave.

John 17:9

"I pray for them. I am not praying for the world but for those You have given Me, because they are Yours."

THE DEEPER QUESTION:

What motivated Rizpah? What example comes to your mind of a mother's great sacrificial love? How do you feel about God's pledge to love you with a greater love than any mother?

_____

_____

_____

_____

_____

_____

_____

_____

_____

_____

_____

_____

_____

_____

_____

_____

_____

_____

Thank You, Lord, for Your great sacrificial love. May I appreciate Your love more each day. Teach me to respond to others with Your kind of love.

Tired of Fighting

2 Samuel 21:15-17

The Philistines were again at war with Israel. David went down with his servants and they fought against the philistines, and David became tired. Ishbi-benob . . . a descendant of the giant . . . said that he would strike David down. But Abishai son of Zeruiah came to David's aid and struck down the philistine and killed him.

I am so thankful God chose to tell us David knew about exhaustion in battle! I need to know that others have experienced the weariness of fighting the same old enemy over and over.

The word for *exhausted* in Hebrew is *uwph*. Doesn't that sound like something you might want to say at the glimpse of an old enemy? It means "to cover, to fly, to faint, to flee away."

Few things make us want to flee more than the prospect of fighting an old battle. The moment that old enemy reappears, we want to run into the nearest forest and never come out.

1 Peter 5:8

Be sober! Be on the alert! Your adversary the Devil is prowling around like a roaring lion, looking for anyone he can devour.

THE DEEPER QUESTION:

When was the last time you wanted to run and hide? What giants do you have to face? How does it feel when your giants keep coming back, and what can you do to slay them?

Father, thank You for taking away some giants in my life and for leaving others. Show me Your purposes in allowing repeat struggles, and teach me to be both faithful and persistent in battle.

Not Mine, But Ours

2 Samuel 23:9-10

Next to him was Eleazar son of Dodo the Ahohite. He was in the Three Warriors with David when they defied the Philistines who had gathered there for battle after the men of Israel had withdrawn. He stood and struck the Philistines until his hand was so tired it froze to the sword. The LORD brought about a great victory that day.

One of the most important truths we can apply from David's ongoing battles with the Philistines is that God will always lead us to victory, but He will lead us His way.

God led David to victory through all four of the battles mentioned in 2 Samuel 21:15-22, but He brought the victory to David through someone else.

I'm sure David's preference would have been for God to make him the hero and leave others in awe over his great strength. God had other plans. He purposely made him dependent on someone else.

Philippians 1:18

What does it matter? Just that in every way, whether out of false motives or true, Christ is proclaimed. And in this I rejoice.

THE DEEPER QUESTION:

Would you rather win victories yourself or be delivered by the valor of others? Why? What risks go along with being considered the hero by other people?

_____

_____

_____

_____

_____

_____

_____

_____

_____

_____

_____

_____

_____

_____

_____

_____

_____

Father, teach me the lesson of humility, that kingdom victories are vastly more important than my personal victories. Teach me to rejoice in the accomplishments of others.

MIGHTY HEROES

2 SAMUEL 23:20-21

Beniah killed the Two warriors of Ariel of Moab, and he went down into a cistern on a snowy day and killed a lion. He also killed an awesome Egyptian: Though the Egyptian had a spear in his hand, Beniah went down to him with only a staff. He took the spear out of the Egyptian's hands, and killed him with his own spear.

God has heroes. If you don't believe it, check Hebrews 11.

You'll only find part of the list there, however, because it just keeps getting longer and longer in heaven. The name of every surrendered person who endures by faith and not by sight is on it.

Having heroes of the faith is perfectly appropriate for us. In fact, I am saddened at the thought of anyone who cannot name a living hero.

Don't let Satan make you cynical. Remember, heroes aren't perfect. They simply live to serve and honor God.

HEBREWS 11:37-38

They wandered about in sheepskins, in goatskins, destitute, afflicted, and mistreated. The world was not worthy of them.

THE DEEPER QUESTION:

Who are some of your present-day heroes in the faith? What makes someone a hero to you? For what character traits would you like to be known?

Lord, make me a person of such faith and character that I would inspire the faith of others. I want to leave faithful footprints for those who follow.

Let's Celebrate!

2 Samuel 22:1-3

David sang the words of this song to the LORD on the day the LORD delivered him from the hand of all his enemies and from the hand of Saul. He said, "The LORD is my rock, my fortress, and my deliverer; He is my God, my rock, in whom I seek refuge; He is my shield and the horn of my salvation, my stronghold."

Nothing is more appropriate than celebrating a victory God has won for us!

After all the ups and downs of David's journey, we get to experience in 2 Samuel 22 the sheer pleasure of attending a celebration. Anyone who has ever experienced victory in Jesus is invited to attend. Someone else just wouldn't understand.

Sometimes God puts a new song in our mouths—a hymn of praise to our God! Other times, He brings us back to an old, familiar song. But it's all worth singing just the same!

2 Samuel 22:20

"He brought me out to an open place; He rescued me because He took pleasure in me."

THE DEEPER QUESTION:

What old victories do you need to celebrate once more? What new victories do you need to celebrate for the first time? How can you make celebration a regular part of your relationship with Christ?

_____

_____

_____

_____

_____

_____

_____

_____

_____

_____

_____

_____

_____

_____

_____

_____

_____

Father, the battles are many. Teach me to daily draw strength from You and encouragement from the battles You have already won.

INTO THE SUNSET

1 KINGS 1:1-2

when King David was old and advanced in years, although they covered him with garments, he could not get warm. So his servants said to him, "Let a virgin maid-servant be sought for my lord the king. She shall serve the king and become his nurse. She will sit in his lap, and my lord the king will get warm."

I am saddened by the initial words of 1 Kings. The words suggest the inevitable to us.

Our David? The one who had killed a lion and a bear? The one who thundered the ground with the frame of an overgrown Philistine? The one who made caves his bed and stole the spear of a savage king? The one who conquered nations and called on the might of heaven?

I am almost shocked by his sudden mortality. As he lay chilled beneath the weight of heavy blankets, we realize his humanity and his frailty. We realize our own.

1 KINGS 1:35

"He shall enter and sit upon my throne. Let him rule in my place. I appoint him to be leader over Israel and Judah."

THE DEEPER QUESTION:

How do you feel about getting older? How does God's presence make a difference in the aging process? How can you better prepare yourself for your old age?

_____

_____

_____

_____

_____

_____

_____

_____

_____

_____

_____

_____

_____

_____

_____

_____

_____

_____

Father, I feel dread at the infirmities of age. Build in me the strength of character not just to finish my race but to finish it well. I want to glorify You all the days of my life.

Now Get Busy!

1 Chronicles 28:9–10

"And you, my son Solomon, know the God of your father, and serve Him wholeheartedly and gladly, for the LORD searches every heart and understands the intention of every thought. If you seek Him, He will be found by you, but if you abandon Him, He will reject you forever. . . . Be strong, and do the work."

David shared with Solomon all that had been gathered for the building of the sanctuary. I find his words so applicable to us today. In essence he said, "I've set aside everything you will need. Now get started."

When I was a little girl, I often remember my mother giving us children various instructions which were received with complaints and questions. She'd finally say, "I've already told you. Now, get busy."

Her words, like David's, were wise and practical. God provides what we need. Now all we need to do is get busy.

1 Chronicles 22:19

"Now set your heart and soul on seeking the LORD your God."

THE DEEPER QUESTION:

What work has God given you to do? What equipment has he given you to complete it? How does seeking the Lord fit into that plan? What, if anything, stands in the way of completing your calling?

Lord, I know You have saved me for good works which You before ordained that I should do. Guide me to do today this day's portion of that work.

A Heart Stilled

1 Chronicles 29:26-29

David son of Jesse was king over all Israel. The length of his reign over Israel was forty years. . . . He died at a good old age, having enjoyed a long life, wealth, and honor; and Solomon his son succeeded him as king. The activities of King David from beginning to end are written in the records. . . .

David's rule ended just as it officially began. His stiffened body bowed before God, with the same abandon he demonstrated when he danced through the streets of Jerusalem.

Was it not he who said, "Bless the LORD, O my soul, and all that is in me, bless His holy name" (Ps. 103:1)? With all that was within him, he had danced.

David's actions were often contradictory, but one consistency wove throughout his life and reign: He was a man of worship, a man after God's own heart.

1 Kings 2:10

David rested with his fathers and was buried in the city of David.

The Deeper Question:

what do you want for your legacy? Will you be known as a person of worship? Will your heart be remembered as beating for God? What lessons most impress you from the life of David?

_____

_____

_____

_____

_____

_____

_____

_____

_____

_____

_____

_____

_____

_____

_____

_____

_____

_____

Father, I want to know You. Give me a heart to know You more. I want to dance down the streets of Jerusalem with You. Give me a heart like David's—a heart like Yours!

Epilogue

One unexpected day, the clouds will roll back and the King of all kings will burst through the sky. Christ Jesus will sit on the throne of David in the city of Jerusalem, and hope will give birth to certainty! We will join the one who said, "You have turned my mourning into dancing; You have removed my sackcloth and wrapped me in joy, so that my spirit will sing praise to You and not be silent." (Ps. 30:11-12). With David, we will sing to One who is Worthy!

That day, there just might be one who can't seem to stop singing. Oh, yes, I believe David will dance once more down the streets of Jerusalem—this time without an eye to despise him. He will be oblivious to everyone but God—the focus of his affections, the passion of his heart.

David will dance his way to that same familiar throne, but this time it will be occupied by Another. No one above Him. None beside Him. David will see the Lord high and lifted up, and His train will fill the temple. He'll fall before the One who sits upon the throne, take the crown from his own head, and cast it at His feet. He'll lift his eyes to the King of all kings, and with the passions of an entire nation gathered in one heart, he will cry, "Worthy!"

Surely God the Father will look
with great affection upon the pair.
All wrongs made right. All faith now sight.
He'll search the soul of a shepherd boy once more
And perhaps He will remark
How very much he has
A heart like His.

SUBJECT INDEX

SCRIPTURE INDEX

The Holman Christian Standard Bible

The Bible is the inspired Word of God, inerrant in the original manuscripts. It is the only means of knowing God's specific plan of salvation and His will for life. Bible translation, both a science and an art, is a bridge that brings God's Word from the ancient world to the world today. In acknowledged dependence upon God to accomplish this task, Holman Bible Publishers presents the Holman Christian Standard Bible,™ a new English translation of God's Word.

Why Another New Bible Translation in English?

There are several important answers to this question:

1. The Bible is the world's most important book, confronting each individual with issues that affect all of life, both now and forever. Since each generation must wrestle in its own language with the message of God's Word, there will always be the need for new translations such as the Holman Christian Standard Bible [HCSB].

2. English is the most rapidly changing language today. The HCSB seeks to reflect many of these recent changes by consistently using modern punctuation, formatting, and vocabulary, while avoiding slang, regionalisms, or deliberate changes for the sake of political correctness.

3. Never before in history has there been as much information about the Bible as there is today—from archaeological discoveries to analysis of ancient manuscripts to years of study and statistical research on individual Bible books. Translations made as recently as ten or twenty years ago do not reflect many of these advances in biblical research. The translators of the HCSB have sought to use as much of this new data as possible.

4. One of the most important developments in the modern world is computer technology. The HCSB has probably used computer technology and telecommunications more than any translation in history. The most advanced Bible software available was used to review the translation at each step in its production.

How Is the HCSB Different From Other Translations?

Translations generally follow one of three approaches to translating the original Hebrew, Aramaic and Greek words of Scripture into English:

1. *Formal Equivalence:* Often called "word for word" translation, formal equivalence seeks to represent each word of the original text with a corresponding word in the translation so that the reader can see word for word what the original human authors wrote.

2. *Dynamic Equivalence:* Often called "thought for thought" translation, dynamic equivalence seeks to translate the meaning of biblical words so that the text makes the same impact on a modern reader that the original text had on its readers.

3. *Optimal Equivalence:* This approach seeks to combine the best features of both formal and dynamic equivalence by applying each method to translate the meaning of the original with optimal accuracy. In the many places throughout Scripture where a word for word rendering is clearly understandable, that literal rendering is used. In other places, where a literal rendering might be unclear in modern English, a more dynamic translation is given. The HCSB has chosen to use the balance and beauty of optimal equivalence for a fresh translation of God's Word that is both faithful to the words God inspired and "user friendly" to modern readers.

Look for these other popular B&H titles by Beth Moore:

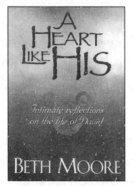

A HEART LIKE HIS
Hardcover 0-8054-2035-5
Audio Book 0-8054-2348-6

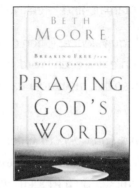

PRAYING GOD'S WORD
0-8054-2351-6

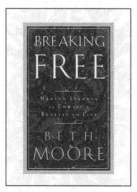

BREAKING FREE
0-8054-2294-3

THINGS PONDERED
0-8054-0166-0